KU-073-450

THE LIFE I NOW LIVE

A true story of adventure and faith in Cambodia

JOELLE KENNY

10 Publishing
a division of **10** of those.com

Unless otherwise stated, Scripture quotations are taken from The Holy Bible, New International Version (Anglicised Edition). Copyright © 1979, 1984, 2011 by Biblica (formerly International Bible Society). Used by permission of Hodder & Stoughton Publishers. All rights reserved. 'NIV' is a registered trademark of Biblica. UK trademark number 1448790.

Scripture quotations marked ESV are from The Holy Bible, English Standard Version, published by HarperCollinsPublishers © 2001 by Crossway Bibles, a division of Good News Publishers. Used by permission. All rights reserved.

Copyright © 2021 by Joelle Kenny

First published in Great Britain in 2021

The right of Joelle Kenny to be identified as the Author of this Work has been asserted by her in accordance with the Copyright, Designs and Patents Act 1988.

All rights reserved. No part of this publication may be reproduced, stored in a retrieval system or transmitted in any form or by any means, electronic, mechanical, photocopying, recording or otherwise, without the prior permission of the publisher or the Copyright Licensing Agency.

British Library Cataloguing in Publication Data
A record for this book is available from the British Library

ISBN: 978-1-913896-64-5

Designed and typeset by Pete Barnsley (CreativeHoot.com)

Chapter illustrations designed by Hannah Li

Cover image adapted from: joshua-newton-xo4B4NaEYQ0-unsplash

Printed in Denmark by Nørhaven

10Publishing, a division of 10ofthose.com
Unit C, Tomlinson Road, Leyland, PR25 2DY, England

Email: info@10ofthose.com
Website: www.10ofthose.com

3 5 7 10 8 6 4 2

The life I now live in the body, I live by faith in the Son of God, who loved me and gave himself for me.

(Galatians 2:20, my italics)

CONTENTS

FOREWORD

Missionaries are not braver or more adventurous than anyone else. How Joelle came to Cambodia from the UK is not a fairy tale, but a real and true story.

In this short book, Joelle honestly shares her struggles and fears, beginning with her challenging childhood. However, Joelle also tells the unfolding story of how God guided her steadily, step by step, as she came to know Jesus Christ personally through the Bible. Since then, she has lived her life by faith, experienced answered prayers and has helped others hear about Jesus in north-east Cambodia.

The Life I Now Live shows that God can use anyone to fulfil his gospel purposes, regardless of their background. God never wastes our life experiences. Rather, he carefully designs our ups and downs for the good of ourselves and others, to his glory.

As you read Joelle's story, I pray that you will find God has a surprising but assured plan for each one of us, and that you would know Christ more personally.

May God guide your life firmly by his steadfast love.

Dr Yuzo Imamura
Field Director, OMF Cambodia

PROLOGUE

'1,2,3,' counted the boy. '4, 5, 6, 7.' A look of horror spread across his face as he reached the last digit.

'This house is bad luck,' he said.

'Is it?' I replied. 'And why is that?'

'My grandma says if the gecko living in your house chirps seven times in a row, then the house is bad luck.'

'Is that so?' I questioned, somewhat amused. 'And who is that?' I pointed to a pair of eyes glaring at me from a dark corner.

'That's Sookie,' he replied, going over to stroke the cat.

'But who does he belong to?'

'He just lives here,' the boy said nonchalantly. 'He's bad luck too. Grandma says all black cats are bad luck.'

When I had seen the boys from next door coming to welcome me into my new home, I had been delighted, but grandma's gloomy superstitions were dampening the mood somewhat.

'He's not bad luck,' said the younger boy. 'Look, there is a small, white mark on one of his feet.' He picked up the cat and held out a paw for us to see.

'Oh phew,' I said. 'So he's not bad luck after all.'

'Where is your family?' the younger one asked.

'I am single,' I answered. 'So it will be just be me living in the house.'

'Aren't you *scared* to live alone?' he asked, gawping at me with huge, brown eyes.

'Scared of what?'

'Scared of ghosts?'

'No,' I chuckled, 'I'm not scared of ghosts.'

I took the cat out of his arms and dangled him in front of my face. 'Hmm, I'm not sure my dogs are going to like *you* living here.' The cat narrowed his eyes and wriggled to free himself from my grip.

What I first noticed about this 'bad luck' house is that when I turned a tap, no water came out. When I flicked a switch, no lights came on. When I plugged in the kettle, no water boiled. To get water coming out of the taps, I first needed to pump water from a well in the yard. But to pump the water, I first needed electricity. I took a look around all the rooms. The house had been empty for many months. It was filthy and stank of mould, but that was nothing a good scrub wouldn't fix – except, of course, there was no water to scrub it with.

The second feature I noticed about my new home was how long, dark and lonely the nights were – especially without any electricity. The landlady had not yet removed the large, wooden statues sitting in the lounge. In the darkness, a laughing Buddha, and some freaky-looking animals, would cast long, spooky shadows across the room. Those first few nights, I pulled my littlest dog, Jimpy, into bed with me and threw the covers over our heads. Maybe grandma *was* right. Maybe this house *was* bad luck. Maybe moving to the furthest, most remote part of Cambodia had all been one *huge* mistake.

1

THE WRONG FAMILY

I was always a fearful child. Not of ghosts or the dark or monsters under the bed, but that people would reject me. Or to be more precise, that they would reject me and my family. In my head, there were strict guidelines that indicated whether your family was acceptable or not. I had a tick list that went something like this. Parents still together – tick. Siblings all have the same father – tick. Stay-at-home mother – tick. Father in full-time employment – tick. Financially secure – tick. A fridge full of food –tick. On this imaginary list, my family barely ticked any of the boxes at all. But every day I went to school and pretended that I came from an ordinary family like everyone else. Until one day – at a Christian youth camp of all places – I was found out.

The camp was organised by the Christian Union at my high school and for the entire time it poured with rain. Not just a sprinkling of rain, but torrential downpours. If my memory serves me correctly, there was very little in the way of teaching or fun activities. Most of the time, us campers were left to entertain ourselves. I was incredibly shy at the age of thirteen and did not know anyone else at the camp, so I remember feeling rather lost and eager for the whole thing to come to an end.

There is one afternoon, though, that I have never forgotten. A group of us were sitting in the mess tent. The rain outside was relentless, and we were bored to tears. This was shown by the fact that there were long, awkward pauses in our conversation. Then suddenly, a girl piped up with a piece of gossip that she was sure would get us talking.

'Have you heard,' she began in an animated

voice, 'that the son of the vicar at St John's Church is dating an *older woman*? *And* she has two kids from previous relationships. The vicar's wife is *furious* about it!'

The girl continued gossiping, but I could no longer hear what she was saying. All I could hear was the pounding of my heart.

That was *my family* she was gossiping about! That '*older woman*' was my mother. *Those kids* were my brother and me.

Something welled up inside me. Before I could take control of myself, I blurted my thoughts out loud. 'That's *my* family you are talking about!' I bellowed.

Everyone fell silent and looked in my direction. I could feel my cheeks burning and my hands trembling. Inwardly, I berated myself for not keeping my stupid mouth shut.

Dating an older woman, who already has kids, may not seem like a big deal today, but it was back in the 1980s. Divorce, living together or having kids before marriage – they were all taboo subjects back then. We sat in a hush for what seemed like an eternity – although, to be fair, it was probably just a few seconds.

It was the gossiping girl who eventually broke the silence. 'I'm sorry,' she said, 'I wouldn't have said anything if I knew it was you.' The poor girl was just as mortified by the whole thing as I was.

I remember little else from that camp. Only the humiliation of that moment. At the tender age of thirteen, what people say about you can be very hurtful and make lasting impressions. I returned home convinced of one thing – no matter how much I *wanted* to be a Christian, I could never truly be one. 'I come from the wrong sort of family,' I told myself. 'Families like mine aren't good enough to be Christians.'

Looking back, I can now see that this somewhat rocky childhood of mine was a fitting prelude to the years God had planned for me overseas. Coming from the 'wrong sort of family' was perfect preparation for the people group God would one day have me serve. God had a plan to use my background in ways I could never have imagined. As for my mother, she would one day learn to love and serve God in remarkable ways and in unexpected places too.

2

EMPTINESS

Surprisingly, despite that miserable camp experience, I still found myself drawn to the Christian girls at school. They seemed comfortable in their own skin, like they knew who they were and were even *content* with who they were. This was appealing to me and I especially enjoyed listening to them talk about their faith. I wanted to hang out with them, and kindly they let me.

Then my years at high school came to an end and I found myself at a university in Birmingham studying visual arts. I was a long way from home and desperate to make new friends. As I was used to having Christian friends, I tried going to the Christian Union in the hope I might make some friends there, but I could not see any recognisable faces. It was hard going to these events alone with no-one to sit with and no-one to talk to. Even at the age of nineteen, I could still be painfully shy at times. I gave up and instead began to socialise with the people I already knew – the people on my course and those living in the same dormitory.

With *this* group of friends, every evening was the same – a couple of beers at the campus bar, then a few more at some dingy nightclub, and then a packet of fish and chips on the way home. Blindly, we all followed the same 'narrative'. A narrative that said, 'Now is the time to live wildly. Don't hold back. Go on, indulge yourself!' And so we did. We got drunk, fooled around with the opposite sex, woke up with hangovers and missed most of our classes. But who cared – we were having fun, *right*? Yes! At first, it was fun. However, as the years rolled on, it became increasingly clear to me that this 'narrative' we had all been wooed by was a false one. I felt starved of meaningful conversations, of purpose and of value. Living for *myself*, for the *moment*, quickly became not the highest point of my life, but one of the lowest and loneliest.

By the end of my third year, I was becoming increasingly restless. I remember one afternoon when a bunch of us sat chatting at the 'boys' house'. One of the photography students began showing us a new book he had purchased. The photos in it were supposed to be 'artistic', but in all truth, they were depraved and pornographic. I knew that if I looked too closely, those repulsive images would be stuck in my mind, so I went to sit on the other side of the room. They noticed I had moved and called me a prude. They thought it was funny to find the vilest images and then shove the book in front of my face. I tried shutting my eyes, but every time I opened them again, the pages were still there in front of me. Everyone fell about laughing.

I am sure they meant no harm by it. But for me, that afternoon was a pivotal moment. In an instant, my mind flashed back to something I once overheard my friend's dad say: 'The Bible tells us to choose our friends wisely. And, of course, the reason God tells us to choose our

friends wisely is because we become like them'
(1 Corinthians 15:33). I looked at the people
around me and asked myself, 'Do I *really* want to
become someone who thinks it is funny to look
at depraved images?'

As my three years at university ended, I had
mixed feelings. Yes, some good memories had
been made. Yes, I cared about the people I had
met and the girls I had lived with. But ultimately,
it had been an empty existence. I envied my
old school friends, whose university experience
had been very different to mine. They had got
involved with a church and had blossomed.
I had gone wild and had … shrivelled. I was
ready to put my student years behind me and
start afresh. But what did 'start afresh' mean? If
I was not going to live to satisfy my own fleshly
cravings, who or what was I going to live for?
And what was the point of life anyway? At the
time, I honestly had no idea!

3

NO MORE REBELLION

After a couple of years had passed since university, I was back in my home town spending time with old acquaintances. I remember a friend, an outdoorsy one, inviting me to go rock climbing the following Sunday.

'I can't.' I replied. 'I have church on Sundays.'

He ignored me and spoke of what fun it was going to be and how many of our friends were going. How I would be a fool not to join in.

'But I have church,' I said, once again. This time a little more firmly.

He huffed and rolled his eyes. 'I'm sure God won't mind you missing church for one week,' he scoffed.

I was taken aback. He was usually so gentle.

'You're right,' I said, equally irritable. 'God wouldn't mind! What I mean is, I *want* to go to church. I like it. I enjoy it. I don't want to miss out.'

He shuffled his feet and avoided my gaze. 'Oh,' he replied.

We stood for a moment in silence.

'So, are you a Christian now then?' he asked, stealing a quick glance at me.

'I don't know,' I replied. 'I'm just … I'm just exploring.'

That first year at church I was on a quest. A quest to understand life. To figure out if 'God' was real or not. And if he was real, to work out what difference did it make anyway? I was not a complete novice; I did have a rough understanding of the Christian message, or 'gospel' as it is commonly called. My understanding of the gospel went something like this: God sent Jesus to die on the cross for our sins. Or to put it another way: God sent Jesus to die on the cross in our place. But now that I began to think, and think *hard*, about it, I was not satisfied with these one-line statements. I needed more information. I remember asking myself, 'What is sin anyway? And why did it deserve *death*?' Was 'sin' a lustful look? A jealous thought? A lie or two? Did these 'sins' *really* deserve death? Wasn't God overreacting a bit?

As I continued in my quest to understand, one small word finally caused the penny to drop. I had heard the gospel taught many times, and in many ways, but for me it was hearing the word 'sin' swapped for the word 'rebellion' that finally made me get it.

The gospel did not begin and end with Jesus dying on the cross. It began all the way back at the creation of the world. 'The earth is the LORD's and everything in it, the world and all who live in it,' says Psalm 24:1. We came from God. We belong to God. He gives us life, breath, and everything we needed to grow and flourish (Acts 17:25). But like ungrateful children, we took his generous gifts and then told him to get lost. 'We will live life without God,' we said. 'We do not want God,' we said. 'We will rule ourselves,' we said. Sin was not just a case of: 'Oops! I slipped up.' It was serious. It was rebellion against our own Creator.

So we decided to go at it alone. To do life without God. What difference did that make? Desperate to understand more, I began reading lots of Christian books aimed at those exploring the Christian faith or new Christians who still had questions. Step by step, I began to see that we were not created for independent living or self-sufficiency. We were created for relationship with God. For dependency on God. To be loved, taught, encouraged, guided, nurtured, strengthened, and counselled – all by him. And so in rejecting God, this world no longer functioned as God had intended (Psalm 81:11–12). Now, our lives, our relationships and our communities were seriously messed up.

I made a bad choice once when I was young. For weeks afterwards, I suffered the consequences of that bad decision. But I did not suffer in silence – I kept on complaining about it. Finally, my mum turned to me and said, 'You've made your bed, now lie in it.' It felt like a cruel thing for her to say, but she was right! And that is exactly what God had the right to say to us. After all, it was our decision to get rid of him and to try to do life without him.

Thankfully, God is more merciful than we are. In his kindness, he longed to give us a second chance. I love the way Romans 6:23 describes this: 'For the wages [or consequences] of sin is death, but the gift of God is eternal life in Christ Jesus our Lord.' This second chance – Jesus dying on the cross to take the punishment our rebellion rightfully deserved – was a kind and generous gift. It was a *free* gift.

I now knew for sure that Christianity was not about being religious, going to church or trying to be a good person. It was not about coming from the 'right sort of family' or having a 'squeaky-clean background' – which was a relief, because I had neither! Nor was it simply an intellectual exercise. Growing in my knowledge and understanding of the gospel had been helpful, but it was still not enough. I had to admit my wrongdoing, open my heart, and let God in.

One evening, as I was driving home from work, I pulled over and sat alone. All around me was stillness and quiet. I took a look across the misty fields and raised my eyes to the darkening sky. It felt as if all creation, in a hushed silence, was waiting for me to do or say something significant. I was tired. I was tired of sitting on the fence. Of showing an interest in God, but then continuing to live *without* him. I wanted a new life. A life *with* God.

'Jesus,' I prayed, 'this gospel message seems to make sense – both of my own heart and of the world I see around me. Of the mess we all are in. If you are real and you are truly there, please help me to know. Please help me believe.' It was a tentative step towards faith, but it was enough to turn my life in a very different direction – a much more exciting and adventurous one.

4

NEW BEGINNINGS

Shortly after my hesitant steps towards faith, I applied to teach at a Christian school in India. I would like to say it was because I wanted to serve God or the children or the people of India, but that would be a lie. I was still too young in my faith for such pious reasons as that. Mostly, I just wanted to do something adventurous – and India sounded like an exotic and interesting place to start.

Hebron School stands high on the peaks of the Nilgiri Hills, a small range of mountains near the southern tip of India. An old steam train winds its way up the mountain to Ooty, a hill station at the very top. I was twenty-five years old when I arrived, and thousands of miles from home, but the next three years would be some of the happiest of my life. I would get to spend my holidays travelling through a desert on the back of a camel or wading through the backwaters of Kerala in a canoe. At school, I would come face to face with a monkey in my bedroom and dive for cover as a herd of buffalo stampeded through the school grounds. Life was just about as crazy as it gets. Yet my most lasting memories are the school staff, a Wednesday Bible study group, and a mini love affair.

The staff at the school were far more mature in their faith than I was and so I took the opportunity to ask them lots of questions about God. Interestingly, they never attempted to answer my questions with their own wisdom. For example, they never said, 'Well, I *think* God is like *this* or that.' Instead, they would open the Bible and show me the answer. They took the time to explain the context of a particular verse and *how* it answered my question. It was so helpful. I remember thinking to myself, 'These Christians actually know who God is and what he is like. They *actually* read the Bible.' I had grown in my understanding of the gospel before coming to India, but I was not yet a Christian who read the Bible regularly. Their love of the Bible and their knowledge of it greatly impressed me, and I hoped that one day I would know it as well as they did.

Similarly, a Bible study group that I attended every Wednesday evening quickly became my favourite part of the week. A few teachers and I would cram into a rickety, old Land Rover and fly off into town for a meeting with some local believers. A different family hosted each week. For us foreigners, this was a real taste of the local culture. Some weeks, we were squished together, sitting cross-legged on a double bed in a tiny, one-room apartment. Other weeks, we were in the lounge of a rather magnificent mansion, with a host of servants fussing over us. But the best part of the evening was always the Bible study itself. Initially, we went through the book of Hebrews. I had never read a whole book of the Bible before and found it fascinating. Each study built upon what we'd learnt the previous weeks, and, over time, we gained a picture of what the whole book was teaching us.

Then I began a love affair and for a moment, life seemed to be just perfect. He was Australian and also teaching at the school. We spent our days off scooting around the mountain on a motorbike and picnicking next to beautiful lakes. It would have been idyllic had there not been some serious flaws, one of which was we struggled to date with purity. As Christians, we knew we must battle against sin and not simply give ourselves over to it. We knew that our bodies were as much the Lord's as our hearts and minds, and so obedience to God was also a physical, bodily affair. Therefore, we didn't sleep together – but we did kiss too much. We struggled to date with purity partly because we were spiritually immature and partly because we had become Christians just before arriving in India. Sadly, old patterns of behaviour do not disappear overnight. It takes time.

I was beginning to learn an important lesson: the purpose of the gospel is not just to *save* us, but also to *transform* us. Faith is not just something you think; it's something you live. I felt we were too young in our faith to enter marriage, so I decided to break off the relationship and instead concentrate on deepening my relationship with God. I left India grateful to God for the three wonderful years he had given me there, but also utterly heartbroken.

5

MATURITY

During my years in India, I had become a true Christian, but that did not mean life was automatically rosy. My dating nightmare had shown me there was still a lot of work God needed to do in my life. If my colleagues in India had taught me anything, it was that the Bible – God's Word to us – is central to a maturing relationship with God. Therefore, the first thing I had to do was find a church that loved God's Word and taught it faithfully. Trustworthy friends recommended a church in London called St Helen's. 'Go to the evening service,' they told me. 'There are lots of people your age.

And make sure you sign up for their mid-week Bible studies.'

That first Sunday at St Helen's, I arrived way too early – it was still forty-five minutes until the service started. A team of people were busily straightening the chairs and putting out Bibles. I shuffled my feet nervously. As I had not seen any coffee shops open nearby and it was too cold to sit outside, I took a seat somewhere in the middle of the church and prepared myself for a long wait. No sooner had I sat down than one of the girls fussing around the church came and plonked herself next to me. I was taken aback by her boldness. 'Hello,' she said, smiling. 'Do you mind if I sit with you?'

Her name was Emily and we chatted merrily until the room filled with people and the service started. Afterwards, she took me to where the coffee and snacks were served and introduced me to all her friends. Everyone was so welcoming. By the time I was leaving to go home, I had arranged to meet Emily the following week at her Thursday night Bible study group. I went as promised, and from that week on, St Helen's was my new church family.

By all accounts, I had made a good start to my new life in London. I had a job. I was settled in a good church. I was enjoying going through John's Gospel with my Bible Study group. There was just one thing stealing my joy: I was still heartbroken. Even though almost a year had passed since I left India, I found myself stuck in an ever-deepening gloom. It was like I had depression. So I asked around at church if there was anyone I could meet for one-to-one counselling.

I was introduced to a lady called Leonie and we began to meet weekly. Her idea of counselling was an interesting one – she took me through an in-depth study of the book of Colossians! I felt kind of cheated and wondered when we were going to talk about *me* and *my* heartbreak, but I was too shy to say anything. By week three, though, I had forgotten my original purpose for meeting with Leonie and just began to enjoy all that we were studying in Colossians. I was learning big truths about the sufficiency of Christ and about God's plan to one day reconcile all things to himself (Colossians 1:15–20). My heartache seemed rather petty in comparison to this big stuff. Diverting my attention to bigger, more important things was obviously the tonic I needed as I began to perk up a little.

During those precious years at St Helen's, I observed that the people most able to trust God with the complexities of life were those in the habit of reading God's Word each day. People would ask one another, 'What are you reading in your quiet times right now?' 'Quiet time' meant time spent reading the Bible alone, and often at home. A typical reply was, 'Oh, I'm going through the book of Psalms' or 'I'm reading Philippians' – or some other book in the Bible. I began to understand that attending a weekly Bible study as well as church on a Sunday was not enough. I needed to draw close to God every single day if I wanted to have an intimate relationship with him. For the first time in my life, I began having a quiet time, reading the Bible alone. This did not happen quite every day at first, but almost so.

I was so grateful for all I was learning about God, in my one-to-ones with Leonie, with my weekly Bible study group and in my quiet times alone. I was like a thirsty sponge, just soaking it all up. 'If only *everyone* got the chance to study God's Word like this,' I sighed to myself one evening. I thought of people I knew who had started on a path towards faith, but who didn't continue on it because they were not studying the Bible. In the end, they all fell away. I pitied them deeply.

I knew in that moment that wherever God took me in life, I must always seek to help others read and understand the Bible. I wanted to help those who had taken a step towards Jesus to stick with Jesus. It was like a fire in my belly – a fire that would keep burning for the next fifteen years and counting. I prayed that evening that God would one day use me to teach the Bible to others. God would answer my prayer, but in an unexpected place and with people of an entirely different language and culture to my own.

6

A TURNING POINT

The plane screeched to a halt at a small, dilapidated building by the runway. This was hardly the international airport I expected for a major city in South East Asia. Cambodia was a busy, chaotic country with a sweaty climate. The first challenge I faced was crossing the road – the volume of motorcycle traffic was unlike anything I had ever seen. The only way to cross was to fix your gaze straight ahead, then step off the curb and slowly glide to the other side, trusting all the motorcycles to swerve expertly around you. It was terrifying, but it worked.

Six months before, back in London, I had started to get itchy feet. My adventures in India had given me a taste for travel and I was keen for more overseas experience. This time, I applied to teach art at a school called Logos, smack bang in the middle of Phnom Penh, the capital of Cambodia.

There was a strange atmosphere in Cambodia – a kind of sadness about the place. The once elegant colonial buildings were now crumbling and peppered with bullet holes. The number-one spot for tourists to visit was a school that had once been used as a torture chamber. It was a nation broken by decades of war. When I spoke to the Cambodians about their turbulent past, I sensed a reticence to hope for anything better. Its most recent tragedy had happened in the late 1970s, when the country fell into the hands of a communist regime called the Khmer Rouge. In the genocide that followed, nearly a third of the population (roughly 2.5–3 million people out of a population of 8 million) were either executed or died of starvation. Thirty years had passed since then, but it was clear the country was still recovering. Its misery overwhelmed me. I felt homesick. I decided to see the year out and then head back to the UK. I told myself that my job until then was just to gut it out.

Then one day as I cycled to school, a lady wearing pyjamas and bunny slippers scooted past me on her motorbike. It made me laugh. Then I noticed there were people all over the city wearing pyjamas. I saw people shopping in the market, taking their children to school, and standing in the queue at the bank all wearing pyjamas. And that was not the only thing that amused me. I saw people riding motorcycles with a fridge or a sofa strapped to their back. Sometimes there was a dog perched on the front of the seat with its paws on the handlebars. That made me laugh because it looked like the dog was the one driving. Cambodia was growing on me. It was sad, but also comical. By the time it was Christmas, I had already agreed to teach at the school for two more years, but for a much deeper reason.

Unlike my years in India, where I had attended an international church, this time I decided to try going to a local Cambodian church. I felt a great curiosity for the Cambodian people, and

I wanted to get to know them better. Going to a Cambodian church worked a treat. I became very close, very quickly, to some very special people. I began hanging out in Cambodian homes, eating Cambodian food, going to Cambodian weddings, and taking trips to the countryside to visit aunts, uncles and cousins.

Making friends with the locals sounds like an obvious thing to do when you live overseas, but it is not. Foreigners living overseas tend to gravitate towards other foreigners and form what is called an expat community. They hang out in places specifically designed for foreigners and eat pizza, hamburgers, and French fries. There is nothing wrong with doing this; I was part of an expat community too. But to befriend people of a different language, culture, and class to your own often takes drive and commitment. It was quite extraordinary, therefore, that for me it happened so easily. I was grateful because it also paved the way for me to start a Bible study group with my new Cambodian friends.

The host of the house we met in was very good at inviting her neighbours to come and study with us. A brother and sister from the house next door came faithfully each week. They asked excellent questions and would stay long after the study had finished to keep discussing the topic. They would then share the things they had been learning with the rest of their family at home. Eventually, their parents and another sibling began joining us too. Two years later, the siblings plus their father decided they wanted to get baptised. Regrettably, though, the mother held back. Over and over, she would say the same thing: 'But what will the neighbours think?' I realised afresh that it took courage to accept Jesus and not care about what people think. And sadly, she lacked the courage necessary. In the end, the family decided to go ahead without her.

Together with my Cambodian church, we went for a picnic in the countryside and baptised all four of them, plus a few others, in a river. The affection I felt for these new believers was extraordinary. I loved them like they were my own family. From that moment on, a kind of 'spiritual motherhood' fell on me. I wanted to protect and nurture their new-found faith with every fibre of my being so that, no matter what, they would stick with Jesus – always.

Shortly after the baptisms, as I contemplated all the wonderful things God had done, I happened to mutter to myself, 'If only I could teach the Bible to Cambodians *full-time.*' It was just a passing thought. But then I began to wonder if it could ever happen. If my church back home agreed to send me here as a missionary – supporting me financially – there was no reason why I couldn't give up my work at the school and instead concentrate on teaching the Bible. The first thing I needed to do was talk to my church back home in London. As I respected their opinion, what they thought of the idea mattered to me. I convinced myself that even if the idea went down like a lead balloon, there was no harm in asking.

At this point, three years had passed since I first came to Cambodia and it was time, for now, to go back to the UK. With a heavy heart, I packed my bags and prepared to leave. The Bible study group came to the airport to see me off. The day before I had given away all my clothing to them, so now here they were at the airport, wearing all my outfits! We waved furiously to each other as I disappeared up the escalator to go through passport control. I had been on the verge of tears, but seeing them dressed in the clothes I had worn every day for the past three years caused me to burst out laughing instead. It was like waving goodbye to numerous replicas of myself. Once again, the Cambodians had turned something sad into something delightfully comical.

7

COLD FEET

'Well, look at that,' I said as the plane touched down at Heathrow. 'Miserable British weather. How lovely to see you again.' I was being genuine. Living and working in a hot climate had not been anything like a two-week holiday in Spain, when you play in a pool all day and eat lots of ice cream. *Working* in temperatures around 40 degrees Celsius every single day is torturous. So, seeing grey skies and that wet, drizzly thing that Britain does so well produced a sigh of relief. Plus, it would be good not to eat rice for a while too. I was most looking forward to eating salmon and mashed potato, so this is

what Mum promised to have ready in the oven
– even though my brother said, 'But salmon
and mash potato aren't even a thing. They don't
go together.'

Shortly after arriving back in the UK, I shared
with my church my ideas about returning to
Cambodia as a mission partner – meaning the
church would take me on as a member of staff
but have me serve in Cambodia rather than on
their own doorstep. They were supportive of the
idea and encouraged me to get further training
so that I could go back equipped to teach the
Bible more effectively. I took their advice and
attended a Bible school for the next three years.
I assumed I would first need to work to raise
the money, but God miraculously provided it
through gifts from others.

Towards the end of my training, it looked
to everyone else that I was all set to go. But I
was not. During my years back in the UK, I had
made new friends. Great friends. Friends that
encouraged me in my faith and were lots of
fun to spend time with. Church and family had
become 'home' to me once again. After years
overseas, I was just beginning to get to know

my niece. What if going back to Cambodia was a huge mistake? What if it destroyed all these precious new relationships? I had what they call 'cold feet'.

I did not tell anyone I was struggling, but instead took some time out to reflect and pray. As I did this, there was one thing I could not ignore. God had miraculously provided all that I had needed to return to Cambodia as a missionary. Three years of Bible training had been generously paid for by others. An organisation called OMF accepted my application to become one of their members, which meant I would work with one of their teams already based in Cambodia. Money that I needed to support myself had come in at the drop of a hat. Friends, and also people I hardly even knew, had committed to pray for me. In addition, both my home church and another London church agreed to send me as one of their mission partners, supplying additional money and support that I needed. Had God not wanted me to go back to Cambodia, he could have closed any one of those doors at any time. But he had not. Returning to Cambodia now became for me not a step of excitement, but a step of obedience. If it were his will for me to go back, then go back I would. I decided to trust God with the relationships I would leave behind. God would be there for them – including my niece – when I could not.

I had packed my bags and waved goodbye to family and friends many times before, but this time it felt different; this move was more serious. I was not going to teach at an international school for a couple of years; I was going to Cambodia indefinitely. I would endeavour to learn the language, make a home for myself, and put down roots. Maybe even get a dog or two. Saying farewell to my mother and brother as I got on the coach to Heathrow was hard. As the coach engine roared to life and we pulled away from the curb, I knew deep down that life would never be the same again. It was a very sobering thought.

I arrived in Cambodia early in the morning, but I was not tired. I was met by some OMF colleagues and taken to the OMF Team Centre – which happened to be in the area I had once lived. After a quick shower and a cup of coffee, I jumped on a bicycle and took a tour of the streets I had once known so well. During that cycle ride, something important happened: I was flooded with a sense of peace. The doubts that just twenty-four hours ago had seemed so strong, simply melted away. I peddled past my old house, my old school, my old coffee shop. I visited a friend and bumped into some of my old school students. Nearly four years had passed, but everyone remembered me and gave me a warm welcome 'home'.

8

NOT MY WILL, BUT YOURS

Although I was happy to be back in Cambodia, those first eighteen months in Phnom Penh were a tough time for me. Various parasites invaded my intestines, but the doctors kept missing my medical problem. I was stuck at home for months on end, too unwell to socialise and with no energy to study. When I did drag myself out, I was grumpy and whinging all the time. I fell behind in my language learning and felt embarrassed that after a year I still could not speak much Khmer (the local language). What was God doing? What was the point of being here if I was sick and useless? How was that helping anyone?

In my lounge, I had a round, bamboo chair with a big, red cushion on it. During my illness, I would sit there for hours, in a comatose state, trying to work out what I should do. I was too sick to work. Should I just give up and go home? As I reflected on my first eighteen months back in Cambodia, I felt ashamed of some of the things I had said and thought. I had come back to Cambodia a proud and presumptuous person who thought that because I had lived in Cambodia once already, I did not need any help or guidance. I was boastful and inwardly critical of missionaries who I considered to be less effective than I had been. Now here I was, weak and useless myself.

In that moment, I realised afresh how dependent I was on God for everything: for my health; for language acquisition; for the perseverance not to give up and go home. God in his wisdom knew that if I was to be used by him, I first needed to depend on his strength and to stop boasting in my own. It was a reminder that God is God, and I am not. I told God I was sorry for my previous attitude and then thanked him for humbling me through this sickness. A few months later, a doctor visiting from Singapore correctly diagnosed my condition. With the right medication, I now began to make a recovery.

With improved health and my language exams finally finished, I took a trip around the country to visit OMF teams working further afield. My heart was set on joining a team based in Phnom Penh, where all my old friends were, but I decided there could be no harm in visiting teams elsewhere. One of my stopovers was in a province called Ratanakiri, in the far north-east of the country and mostly inhabited by hilltribe people. The OMF team working there were involved with two tribes in particular: the Krung and the Brao.[1]

During my stay, we travelled from village to village visiting some of the hilltribe believers. The roads were hilly, mud tracks and very slippery. Every time we ventured over some rickety, old bridge, I would close my eyes and clench my teeth

---

[1] See Appendix on page 103: The Krung and Brao

until we safely reached the other side. The houses in the villages were raised on stilts and made of either bamboo and thatch or wood. Inside, there was nothing much above floor level – no tables or chairs or beds or wardrobes, just a woven mat that they rolled out to either eat on or sleep on. They cooked crouched on the floor over a wood fire and steamed their rice in woven baskets.

The hilltribe people were not Buddhist like the rest of Cambodians were, but Animist. They believed that spirits lived in the trees, the air, and the water; that these spirits controlled the harvest, the wind and the rain; and that the spirits communicated their displeasure through nightmares, accidents, sickness and crop failure. According to the people, the only way to keep the spirits happy and out of mischief was to offer them a blood sacrifice – a chicken, a pig, or a much-prized buffalo. So the people raised animals not to eat, but to sacrifice. It was a deeply costly affair for them.

One time, I went foraging in the forest with some of the Krung women. We wore baskets on our back and went in search of anything edible, like bamboo shoots, leaves and low-hanging fruit. But we also cut down a banana tree and dragged the trunk home with us. I was perplexed. The tree had no fruit on it, and I could not think what they wanted the trunk for. Then I watched as they sliced up the trunk, boiled it with a little salt and pepper, and then served it with a bowl of steamed rice. It was delicious.

The OMF workers in Ratanakiri were praying for someone to come and work with the Krung and the Brao youth. I could see the need. Young people were becoming Christians, but there was no-one walking alongside them in their faith. I hoped they would find someone, but I knew for sure that person was not me. Firstly, Ratanakiri did not have a supermarket. That meant no bread, pasta, milk, tea, and other essentials. Secondly, it did not have any air-conditioned coffee shops – which were my only escape from the stifling heat. And thirdly, I did not want to be a youth worker. I had met youth workers before. They were extroverts who loved goofing around, playing games and throwing pizza parties. I was an introvert and far less energetic. I made it quite clear – both to myself *and* to God – that I would never, ever serve in a place like Ratanakiri. It was fascinating to visit, but to live and work in – no thanks!

God, on the other hand, would not let the idea go. As is often his way, he kept bugging me until I stopped to reconsider what I was trying to run away from. Whilst washing the dishes, I would find my mind wandering yet again to the people I had met back in Ratanakiri. Every time I met missionaries working with young people in Phnom Penh, my heart would cry out, 'You should be working with the youth in Ratanakiri. They *really* need someone like you.' I felt a burden for the young people there, and the burden had grown to such an extent that I could no longer ignore it. Slowly, in the background, God was chipping away at my heart. If no-one else was willing to go and work with the youth in Ratanakiri, maybe it needed to be me. One morning, as I drank my coffee and read my Bible, I found myself making a deal. 'Right, Lord,' I said, 'You win. I will go back to Ratanakiri for a second visit. This time for longer. And we'll see how I feel after that.'

I kept my promise and made another visit. During that time, I finally surrendered myself to

God's desire for me. On the bus back to Phnom Penh, as I watched the countryside zooming past the window, I found myself saying, 'OK, Lord, not my will, but yours' (Matthew 26:39). I was learning something big: if Jesus could trust his Father right up to his death on the cross, I needed to trust God with everything too – both in the place he would have me serve him and in the role he would have me do. Six months later, I left behind the comforts of the city – its paved roads, supermarkets, and air-conditioned coffee shops – and headed to the jungles of the far north-east.

Shortly after my departure for Ratanakiri, my mother, now a committed Christian herself, came to teach at a school in Phnom Penh for missionary children. God had a sense of humour because though we were now both in Cambodia, we were as far from each other as Scotland is from London. Incredibly busy with our new jobs, we still only saw each other once or twice a year!

9

NOT ALONE

After a twelve-hour-long journey from Phnom Penh, finally I arrived in Ratanakiri. A few days after I arrived, a couple of boys from the house next door ran to greet me. They followed me through the gate, chattering enthusiastically about the previous tenants, who were also foreigners. As I fumbled with the key to open the front door, the older boy stopped chattering and began counting: '1, 2, 3, 4, 5, 6, 7.' He was counting the chirping of a resident gecko. Not the little ones that run frantically around the walls, but the large kind with heads the size of a small fist. They like to hide in a dark spot –

behind a fridge, for example – and then frighten the life out of you by poking out their ugly head when you're least expecting it.

'This house is bad luck,' the older boy said once he had finished counting. 'My grandma says if the gecko living in your house chirps seven times in a row, then the house is bad luck.' I couldn't say if the house was 'bad luck' or not, but it was certainly filthy and in need of a good scrub.

We had dumped the furniture from the pick-up truck under the eaves of the house so I could first get the house cleaned. Then I discovered there was no water or electricity. How could I clean the house without running water? I decided the best thing to do was wait until the plumbing and electrics were sorted, and the house was sparkling clean, before moving in the furniture. In the meantime, I threw together some blankets and cushions for a makeshift bed, and waited for the landlady to appear with an electrician. It took five long days for her to come, and my patience was sorely tested!

The relentless rain did not help. Every year in Ratanakiri the heavens open and pour with rain for a few months (usually from July to November). They call this a 'monsoon' or the 'rainy season'. Foolishly, I moved to Ratanakiri towards the end of July, and it bucketed with rain every single day. I watched in horror as the lane outside my house turned into a river flowing with mud. Not only was it dangerous to drive, but it was lethal even to step out of the gate. Just about every day I would slip and become covered from head to toe in bright red mud. The boys next door found it highly amusing. I found it exasperating. I was beginning to think grandma was right – maybe this house was bad luck after all.

Then I started working in a village called Ochum and things got harder still. I went there to study the Bible with the youth and the women, but they were only free to meet in the evenings, which meant driving home late at night. With no streetlamps, it was hard to see the road in the heavy rain. I would drive all the way back at 20 mph, squinting to see where the sharp bends were so I did not veer off the road. My hands would keep slipping as I then fumbled to open the front gate in the pouring rain. Then Topsy and Turvy, my two larger dogs, would dash out into the road to play. Soaked to the skin, I would chase them down the lane, trying to coax them back home again. It wasn't funny; it was tiresome.

Two months after my arrival, Nah, one of the sweet young ladies I studied the Bible with at Ochum, was killed in a road accident. That felt like a punch in the guts. The funeral lasted five long days. On the fifth day, I returned home exhausted, sat on the floor and wept. I hated it here. I hated the mud, the rain, the dark, the driving home late at night. And now dear, sweet Nah was gone. It was all too much. I needed God to comfort my weary and tired soul. I needed to know he was with me. I needed to know he cared. I needed the courage to carry on. 'Please show me I'm not alone, God,' I prayed. 'Please show me you are here. Please show me you are with me.'

A couple of days later, as I ran up the stairs to my balcony, I caught sight of the spirit house in my yard. It was a large, posh, concrete one, with a shelf to put food offerings and an incense burner. Whereas the Krung people made sacrifices to the spirits, Buddhist people built little houses for them where they were supposed to dwell. Every property owned by a Buddhist person had one. A Christian friend was adamant I should tear down the one in my yard, saying that Christians visiting the house would not approve of it. But another Christian lady was adamant I should leave it: 'If you tear it down, and then a neighbour gets sick or a grandparent dies, they will blame you. They will say it's because you tore down the spirit house.' I imagined grandma next door waiting for me to tear it down and then popping her clogs on purpose, just so everyone would blame me.

I was not scared of the spirit house. I didn't believe it had the power to harm me or to kill grandma. But I was in a dilemma about it. Two months had already passed and still I had not made up my mind. As I continued running up the steps to my home, I sighed and said out loud, 'Lord, I still don't know what to do about that spirit house. So, I'm just going to do nothing and leave you to sort that one out.' It was one of those throwaway prayers you make whilst on the go. The kind of prayer you don't expect God to take seriously.

A couple of days later, I heard an enormous crash in the yard. I ran on to the balcony in a panic. My cleaner's son stood in the yard with a sheepish look on his face. Next to him was the spirit house, smashed to smithereens. 'I'm sorry,' he began to sob. 'I was climbing the fence. I put my foot on the spirit house to steady myself. It fell and smashed.'

I laughed and laughed and clapped my hands together in glee. God was *so* clever! The spirit house was gone, and no-one could blame me; it had happened in an accident. I ran over to the boy and tried to comfort him. 'It's OK,' I said. 'I am not angry. I'm delighted!'

As I clambered into bed that night, my mind was still buzzing from the day's events. God had answered my prayer. He had shown me I was not alone. He had shown me he is never too busy elsewhere. He never has his back turned. He is never absent. 'He even knows the number of hairs on my head!' I said to myself, with a grin on my face (Matthew 10:30). I had found the courage to carry on.

10

A HOUSE
OF BLESSING

Those first two years in Ratanakiri, I had the unexpected privilege of sharing my house with a radio project called 'Source of Life'. This was a Christian radio programme broadcast in three of the local languages: Krung, Jarai and Tampuan. As I lived on the top floor of the house and rarely used the rooms on the ground floor, I offered that space for them to use as a recording studio. I hardly knew at the time what I was letting myself in for. The once quiet house quickly became a hive of activity!

Krung people from all over the province began arriving at the property. They came to record songs, testimonies, and portions of the Bible in their own languages. Sometimes, a group would come and stay for several nights, and my yard would become a little village of its own. I would sit on the balcony in the mornings with a mug of coffee and watch with fascination the scene below. Babies would be swinging in hammocks and pots of food would be bubbling over wood fires. My three dogs loved all the coming and going. Topsy and Turvy enjoyed the extra scraps of food. Jimpy, my little, fluffy dog, enjoyed all the extra fuss and attention.

In the mornings, I joined the radio staff for their time of worship. We studied the Bible, sang, prayed, and shared testimonies. It was a good chance to practise my Khmer and more interesting than a boring old language lesson. My favourite part was hearing stories about the programme's listeners. If they had questions or wanted to chat, they could call the studio and have a private conversation once the live broadcast had stopped. Families living in remote villages – where quite possibly no Christian had ever set foot – were calling to say they wanted to become Christians. Those involved with the radio project tried their hardest to follow up every single call. It was an incredibly exciting time for us.

Once, a family from the Jarai tribe phoned in. They told the Jarai producer that they had been listening to the show for many months now and felt ready to become Christians. There was just one problem: they had never met a Christian before, so what did it 'look like' to be a Christian? What things should they do differently? What were the Christian customs and practices? These were understandable questions for them to ask. Thom, a Jarai man who worked part-time for the radio programme, volunteered to go and find the family. He drove his motorbike for miles in search of their village. When he found them, he entered their home and began teaching them from the Bible. Encouraged by their sincere desire to know God, he made several more visits. Soon a large group of people were gathering there to listen to Thom teach. Next, Thom scoured the local area in search of another Christian family, finding one in a village not too far away. He introduced the two families and encouraged them to meet on Sundays for worship. They did as he suggested and that was the beginning of a new church.

The effect of these radio broadcasts on other listeners only emerged much later. Fast forward five years to 2020 and a new missionary couple from India arrives in Ratanakiri to do pioneering work. They want to work in a village that still has no Christians and choose a village belonging to the Tampuan tribe. The husband has only visited the village a handful of times when there are already several people interested in becoming Christians. The man is perplexed. How are these people ready to accept Jesus? How had they even heard of him? The reply is always the same: for years now, they have been listening to a Christian radio show broadcast in their own language. In their hearts, they are willing and ready to know Jesus. They are just waiting for someone to come and help them *get started*. The couple are blown away by this and excitedly share their story with the producers of the radio show and with the rest of the missionary community. The story is a great encouragement to us all.

The house of 'bad luck' was now a house of blessing. From within its walls, a message of hope and forgiveness had spilled out across the airwaves. A message that over the next five years and counting would be warmly received by many.

11

BOYS WANTED

'Why aren't you at school today?' my colleague asked some children as he walked through a village.

The children were filthy and dressed in rags, but their poverty did not stop them from being bright and cheerful. 'We went to school,' one of the boys shouted, 'but the teacher sent us home again.'

'Why?'

'He said he was too lazy to teach us today.'

I had to chuckle when I heard this. I tried to imagine a teacher in the UK doing the same thing – boy, would that teacher be in trouble!

Sadly, it is a common story in Ratanakiri. Krung children are out of school more often than in. In addition, education in hilltribe villages usually stops at the end of primary school. As a result, most of them finish their schooling around the age of ten and never became fully literate adults.

I was relieved that the youth in a village called Ochum *did* have access to a middle- and high-school education because it was the first place I hoped to start a youth group. If the youth there could already read, studying the Bible would be a lot less challenging.

The youth group in Ochum were all girls – just six or seven of them – and we decided to meet together on Friday nights. As I did not yet know enough of the Khmer language to teach competently, I needed a creative way of leading the girls through a Bible lesson. I decided to choose a Bible passage and then use my language lesson that week to prepare written questions that would help the girls think more deeply about the passage. On the night that we met, I would ask one of the girls to read the passage from the Bible and then the questions. The girls would then discuss the questions in their own language before giving me a summary of their thoughts in Khmer. Next, I would add my own comments in my limited Khmer. The whole process sounds awkward, but working in a language that is not your own *is* awkward. I had to learn to accept my limitations and trust God to be at work all the same. And this little method of ours worked surprisingly well; the faith of the girls was definitely growing.

Within a year or so, my Khmer had improved and I was able to teach the girls without their help. But my primary goal was still to equip the girls to be able to teach the Bible themselves and lead such groups. It was not good for the local Christians to become too dependent on missionaries. So I decided to prepare a rota in which, every week, different people were leading either a game, the singing or the Bible lesson. There were four girls I chose who I felt were capable of teaching a Bible lesson. Including their names alongside my own on that particular rota was sneaky of me and I wondered how they would react. Yet when I showed the girls the rota, they were incredibly brave and agreed to give it a go.

On the first night of our new rota, I was nervous to see what would happen. That first week, they would lead everything, and I would do nothing! I was relieved to discover everyone had come prepared to do their bit. The girls teaching the Bible lessons soon became very good at this. (In fact, in 2019, two of those girls – Mei and Perl – became the first-ever people from the Krung tribe to go to Bible school.)

There was just one thing that continued to discourage us: there were still no boys in the youth group, and therefore, it was not growing. Every week, we prayed for boys to join us. Some weeks, a boy or two would drop in, but they never stuck with it. After two years had passed since the youth group began, I resigned myself to the fact that we would probably always remain a little group of ladies.

The time had now come for me to go back to the UK for 'home assignment'. This is when OMF team members are required to go home every four years to reconnect with church and family. I would be gone for one whole year. I encouraged the girls to keep meeting without me and left them with study materials to help them prepare Bible lessons. I wondered what I would find when I came back. Would the girls have continued meeting? Would they still be going strong in their faith? Or would some of them have fallen away? All I could do was keep praying for them.

A couple of the girls now had smartphones, so although we were in different parts of the world, we kept in touch via social media. A few months after I had left, they began posting photos of the Friday night meetings. The group had grown. And I could see boys in the photos. Lots of them. Six months later, I counted thirty-five young people in just one photo. I waited for the numbers to drop again, assuming it was just a fad, but they didn't. Then I saw photos of the boys in a church football club called 'Peaceful FC' that they had formed. I couldn't believe what I was seeing – since I had left, the youth group had quadrupled in size and now even had its own football club. I was baffled –how could this have happened? I soon found out.

Whilst in the UK, I kept coming across people who were praying for the youth at Ochum. Surprisingly, most of them were people I had never even met before. I was also told of one lady who, overwhelmed by prayer letters from missionaries, had decided to pray consistently for just one thing: our youth group! I knew without a doubt that the group was growing because God was answering prayers. I realised that prayer partners, even those thousands of miles away, had a direct impact on our work. My appreciation of them rocketed. They were the backbone of our ministry, and I was determined to never forget that.

I returned to Cambodia a year later, excited to see this utterly transformed youth group. I watched in wonder as a steady flow of people kept arriving through the door. The boys, with big grins on their faces, were rowdy and playful. Would they settle down when the Bible lesson began or be disruptive? When the lesson did start, a hush fell on the room. The boys became quiet and attentive. They participated in the discussion and asked brilliant questions. I was left with no doubt that their new-found faith was sincere.

The youth group had grown both in numbers and in understanding whilst in the care of just four young women: Mei, Perl, Sinet and Marie. I was so very proud of them! And I could see God's wisdom in the growth happening whilst I was away. The Krung Christians needed to see that this growth was not the work of a missionary, but God at work through *them*.

12

BRAVE WOMEN

Although the main reason for me coming to Ratanakiri was to work with youth, I could see there was also a great need for someone to work with the Krung women. A women's Bible study group was already meeting in Ochum, but not in any other Krung villages. Having discovered that there was a good number of Christian women in a village called Krala, that seemed the perfect place to get a second group started. When I asked those women, they were very keen on the idea.

The women at Krala were different to those in Ochum. Their lives were much harder. Though intelligent women, they had never had the opportunity to go to school, so the majority were illiterate. A good number of them were also elderly and hard of hearing. Nor were the ladies used to hearing Khmer spoken with a foreign accent. Some found it hard to follow my lessons. Teaching these women was a privilege, but also a challenge. We needed to find a way of overcoming these obstacles – but how?

I noticed that one of the younger ladies could understand me better than the others. Her name was Moich. So when everyone looked lost, I would ask Moich to reteach that part of the lesson in their own language. Soon, she was reteaching parts of the lesson without me even asking her to do that. Sometimes, she would go over to one of the deaf ladies and shout a summary of what we had been learning in their ear. I liked watching Moich teach – she was bold and did it very well. Now that I had a 'helper', we began to make good progress.

Poverty and a lack of education were not the only hardships for the women at Krala. Most of their husbands were not Christians, so their new-found faith had caused tensions in the family. One woman, Sabring, suffered more than the rest. She was a disabled lady who, leaning heavily on a bamboo stick, dragged a lame leg behind her. Her husband was fond of drinking. He drank heavily whenever he went to a wedding, funeral, or sacrifice. Then he would return home drunk and aggressive, and frighten the family. Drunkenness was a trait within the culture that needed transformation, just as it did in my own culture back home. Tears would form in the corner of my eyes whenever Sabring told me of his drunken abuse, and yet, as a rule, she was always cheerful and smiley – I deeply admired her faith and resilience.

Sadly, things got worse for Sabring. One day, when she was out foraging for food, she became dizzy and passed out. When she came to, she was completely paralysed. Eventually, her family found her and carried her home. After several days had passed, she still could not move, eat, or drink unaided. When I heard what had happened, I drove Sabring to the local hospital. She stayed there a week, but the doctors were unable to diagnose her condition or do anything to help her. So I packed her bags and took her home again.

Back at home, Sabring's relatives muttered aloud, 'She'll not last long. She'll be dead in two weeks. Just you see.' I was shocked. There was no need for Sabring to die. She was still only forty years old. They just needed to care for her properly. I busied myself finding a wheelchair, a commode, nappies for adults, a comfortable mattress, and a pillow. Then I instructed the whole family on how to care for Sabring. I told them I would visit again in three days' to see how things were going.

When I returned, I found Sabring lying face down on a urine-soaked mattress. She was groaning, dehydrated and very poorly. I turned her over, cleaned her up and made her drink lots of water. Then I ordered some boys to go and find some bananas, so I could mash them up and feed her. I had noticed that outside her home were the remnants of a sacrificed pig. Instead of caring for Sabring those past three days, her husband had made a sacrifice, got drunk and completely ignored her needs. His neglect had almost killed her. Now the relatives were outside discussing getting a coffin ready. I could tell Sabring was losing the will to live. So I posted on social media an urgent appeal for prayer. Then I pleaded with the women at the Bible study group to visit Sabring every day. I asked them to feed her, bathe her and pray with her. They agreed to do all they could to help.

I was relieved to hear through the grapevine a couple of weeks later that Sabring had improved. It was even rumoured she could move the leg that had been lame for ten years – but I convinced myself I must have misheard that bit. I decided it was time to make another visit.

As I got out of the car, I could see Sabring sitting upright, combing her hair. She had an enormous grin on her face. 'Look,' she said, 'I can move my leg.' She wriggled her toes and kicked the previously lame leg. My jaw dropped open. It was true – *she could move it!* I sat next to her on the bamboo platform under her house and begged her to tell me everything.

'The neighbours have been asking which sacrifice made me well,' she said. 'I tell them this: when my family made a sacrifice to the spirits, I felt hopeless and wanted to die. But then the church began to visit me and pray for me. And suddenly, I felt encouraged and I wanted to live.

It was their prayers to Jesus that helped me get well, *not the sacrifice.'*

Sabring had not recovered completely. She was still limited in her movement; she still needed to use a wheelchair. But she was recovered enough that she could now feed herself – *and therefore keep living!* I showed Sabring my posts on social media and listed all the countries where people had been praying for her. She marvelled that people who had never even met her cared enough to pray. Her miraculous recovery was now the talk of the village. Sabring had a story to tell; a story of God's goodness to her. And the brave woman that she was, she did not shrink from telling it.

13

MORE SURRENDER, GOD?

After two years of living and working in Ratanakiri, I now felt settled and in a good routine. Working with the youth and women out in the villages was a fulfilling and enjoyable role. I had even heard rumours that a supermarket and a Thai brand of coffee shop called Amazon were coming our way. I was looking forward to the day I could buy cheese, yoghurt, and an ice-cold, caramel frappe. All in all, life in Ratanakiri was ticking along just fine. Things were under control and manageable; I felt capable and effective. Until, that is, God decided to shake things up a bit.

One of the problems facing the Krung youth was that most of their villages only provided a primary school education. If anyone wanted to study beyond primary, they needed to leave home and find dormitory accommodation in the district town of Banlung, where I lived. There were already Christian-run dormitories for boys, but none for girls. In the space of two weeks, three separate groups of people asked me if I would consider opening a dormitory for girls – not instead of my work out in the villages, but in addition to it. My external reply was, 'Oh, what a lovely idea. Let me think about it.' But my internal reply was, 'No, I can't. Go away and leave me alone!'

I would love to write that I joyfully agreed to deny myself, take up my cross and follow God's leading (Mark 8:34), but that would be a lie. Stubborn mule that I am, I did the opposite and went to God with my list of objections. 'Lord, have I not made enough sacrifices already? I gave up my friends and family to come to Cambodia. Then I gave up friends in

Phnom Penh to come to Ratanakiri. I agreed to do youth work, even though that was something I never envisaged myself doing. Do I now need to give up my own home too? Do you really mean for me to *surrender everything*?' I reminded God that I was an introvert. That for the sake of my sanity, I needed my own space, my privacy. How could I do that with a house full of teenage girls? In my hasty response, I had forgotten that God already knew me; that he was the one who had made me. Truth be told, what I really wanted was the 'glory' of being a missionary without the 'cost'. I craved the 'applause' without the 'sacrifice'.

It was no coincidence that when I was asked to consider opening a dorm, I was also reading the book *On Being a Servant of God* by Warren W. Wiersbe. God gently reminded me through that book that when he calls us to serve him in a particular way, he does not then leave us to carry it out alone. He freely gives all that we need to fulfil the task he asks us to do. In Colossians 1:29, Paul says of serving God, 'For this I toil, struggling with all his energy that he powerfully works within me' (ESV). Paul describes serving

God as toil and struggle, meaning it's hard work! But then he goes on to describe that such service is possible because God's energy or strength is powerfully at work within him.

I still had my doubts about running a girls' dorm. It felt like a challenging role. I thought back to my own teenage years – the fluctuating hormones, the mood swings, the shyness, the jealousy, the friendship and boyfriend troubles. Was I really cut out for this job? No, I wasn't, but that passage in Colossians convinced me it was good to attempt things beyond myself. Things I cannot do without God's help. Things that would cause me to rely on his strength and enabling more and more.

On 31 October 2018, the radio project moved out of my house into a purpose-built recording studio. The makeshift studio they had assembled in my home had run its course. They needed a bigger, better space, and God had provided the funds necessary for them to build a permanent 'home' of their own. I did not have the time to process the end of an era or to mourn their loss; early the next morning, eight dorm girls landed on my doorstep.

The dogs signalled their arrival with a chorus of barking. It was only 7.00 a.m. and I hadn't even finished my coffee! I stepped on to the balcony and waved for the girls to come in. Each girl was clutching a bag of rice, a couple of pumpkins and a mini backpack of belongings. I thought of how when I left home to go to university, we crammed the car full of stuff – a kettle, a rug, a TV, towels, bedding, crockery, a hairdryer, a bed lamp, and tons of clothing. Their one tiny bag of belongings seemed pitiful in comparison. I knew it was most likely all they owned. A wave of shame washed over me as I realised once again how rich and privileged I was to be born in the West. But there was no time to dwell on that thought – the girls had arrived, and I needed to go and welcome them into their new home.

A NEW POWER?

14

A NEW FAMILY

Although I could accommodate more than eight girls, I decided to keep the number low so that we functioned like a family rather than an institution. I also decided to take girls who were already involved with a church back home. I hoped that by investing in the girls spiritually, they might one day become very helpful, active members of the church – leading youth groups, women's groups, and Sunday schools.

My next decision was to employ a local person to help oversee the dorm. The girls needed a role model – not a foreigner like me, but a local woman like them. I employed a lady called Yeat, who was from the Tampuan tribe, a very strong Christian, and a wonderful Bible teacher. She was absolutely perfect for the role and the girls just loved her.

Those first few weeks that the dorm opened were a learning curve for all of us, but particularly for the girls. Living in a purpose-built house, complete with running water, electricity, and a fridge, was a big adjustment for them. They knew what a fridge was, but they had never used one before. Some of the girls were intrigued by the magnets on the fridge door. They pulled them on and off, perplexed by the force that sucked and held them there. Others played with the freezer compartment, opening and shutting the door to feel the cool steam on their face. When I saw one of the girls putting eggs in the freezer compartment, I realised I needed to teach the girls how to use a fridge properly.

'This part keeps things cold,' I explained, pointing to the fridge itself. 'And this part,' I continued, indicating the freezer section, 'turns things to ice. If you want to eat the food from the part that turns things into ice, you need to let it melt first. Salad and eggs should not be turned to ice. They should be kept in the cold part only.'

'Oh,' said the girls in unison, nodding their heads.

One afternoon, I found Yeat, my dorm helper, prodding a block of cheese with a confused look on her face. 'What is this? she asked. 'Is it soap? Why have you put soap in the fridge?'

'No,' I laughed, 'it's cheese. We eat it. It tastes good. Do you want to try some?'

'No,' she said, with a look of disgust on her face. 'It stinks!'

Living in a house with a bathroom was another first for the girls. Back in their villages, the girls bathed in a river or at the local well. They would wrap a sarong around themselves and pour water over their heads using a plastic beaker. So every evening, the dorm girls would gather in the bathroom to bathe in a group, just as they would at the river. I could hear, over the sound of splashing water, the girls laughing and playfully bickering with each other. It made me smile. I decided not to tell them that the normal way to use a bathroom was to bathe alone with the door shut because I didn't want to ruin all the fun they were having.

Every evening, at 7.00 p.m., the girls, Yeat and I would gather together for a time of worship and a Bible lesson. I wondered how the girls would react to this daily fixture. Would they find it tiresome and boring? Would it be too much for them after a long day at school? Would they feel it was something being forced upon them? Would they resent it? To my delight, the girls seemed to genuinely enjoy the meetings. Even if one of the girls was sick and permitted not to come, they would still drag themselves out of bed to join us. They didn't want to miss out! It was not just a time of study, but also a time of bonding and laughter, and an opportunity to support and encourage each other. It was our 'family time together' and we all looked forward to it.

15

MESSY LIVES

When I decided that I wanted to open a dorm explicitly for girls involved with a church, I assumed the girls would come from the families of church leaders or of Bible translators who were helping to translate the Bible into the local languages. Surely these were the type of Christian families that would send their daughters to stay in our dorm? I was wrong about that.

In the first week that the dorm opened, wanting to encourage the girls to share a bit about their background, I asked them how we could be praying for their families. It turned out only two of the girls came from Christian families where both parents were already believers. The rest of the girls had either one or both parents who were not Christians. Asking how we could pray for their families was like opening a floodgate. One by one, the girls bravely shared some things that were hard to talk about.

Some of them had fathers who were making their lives a misery. Their dads drank heavily and were easily enraged, causing the whole family to struggle under their constant abuse. Another girl shared how two years ago her father had taken his own life. Then another shared how her uncle, whilst high on drugs, had chased her out of the house with a machete, threatening to 'cut her up'. This wasn't a funny story; he had meant it and she had been very frightened by the incident.

None of their stories were new. I knew some of the locals had drinking problems. I knew that drugs were a big issue too. I knew families were often too poor to feed themselves. I knew that amongst the Krung people, there was a high rate of suicide. I just hadn't expected these lovely, sweet Christian girls to have those backgrounds. It was sad and shocking. Sat in a circle on the floor, we poured out our hearts in prayer. We held hands tightly and prayed together in unison. I could feel the tears welling up in my eyes. This home was not just a place that enabled girls to finish school; it was a refuge. A place where the girls were safe. A place where they could take a rest from the brokenness at home and be loved and encouraged.

I remembered how, as a child, I thought I could never be a Christian because I came from the 'wrong sort of family'. Now here I was, a missionary, in a home full of girls who came from the 'wrong sort of families'. I knew what it was like to live in a home of fear and violence. A home of broken dreams and tense relationships. And because I knew, I could sympathise and understand. I didn't know back then that my childhood would stand me in good stead for the years to come in Asia. That my childhood would be a fitting prelude to the people I would one day serve in Cambodia. The girls' lives were messy, but I also knew that God could take messy lives and heal and transform them – just as he had done with mine. I was living proof that with God in the picture, no situation is ever hopeless.

EPILOGUE

Two years after I opened a girl's dorm in my house, a deadly virus called Covid-19 took the world by storm in 2020. Schools were shut down and people were ordered to lock themselves away at home until the virus was under control. Even my work out in the villages was temporarily put on hold. The dorm girls were ordered to return to their homes. We did not know when we would next see each other – possibly not for a long while.

We held hands and prayed together one last time. Then the girls hopped on motorcycles, three per vehicle. One of the girls was wearing pyjamas. To this day, people out and about in their pyjamas still makes me smile. I stood outside to wave them off. As they pulled away, they turned their heads and waved a hearty farewell. 'Goodbye teacher, Goodbye,' they shouted.

While one of the girls turned her head, her gaze lingered. She looked me straight in the eye and gave a sad little smile. It was her way of telling me that she loved me, as I loved her.

'Lord,' I prayed, 'thank you for giving me these precious girls. Please watch over them and keep them safe. Please keep their faith in you strong.'

I walked back into the house and paused for a moment. It felt quiet and empty. For the past four years, my home had been a hive of activity – first with the radio studio and then with the dorm girls. Now it was just me and the dogs again. The silence was eerie, as though it were loitering in the wrong place; my home was a place God designed for laughter and movement. I inhaled deeply and looked at the four walls encircling me. Within these walls, God's Word had been studied, sung, and lifted up and out into the airwaves. It was quite remarkable what God had done here – especially after the gloomy predictions of 'bad luck' at the start!

I sat on the floor and beckoned the dogs to come for a snuggle. I buried my face in their fur, stroked their heads, and felt comforted by the sound of their warm, beating hearts. I did not know what lay ahead. What God would do with this new season of stillness and quiet. A time of reflection perhaps? A time to reflect on the life I now live – or, to be more precise, the life I now live by faith in God. What a journey it has been. What an adventure. So many twists and turns. So many ups and downs. And yet all of them have been so carefully crafted for the good of myself and others.

I thought back to my own teenage years. The plans I once had for myself. The dreams I once dreamed. If I could go back and speak to my teenage self, what would I say to her? I would advise, 'Whatever plans you have for yourself, whatever dreams, tear them up and throw them away. For it is *nothing* compared to the life God has planned for you. The life you now live by faith in God *far* exceeds it all.'

DISCUSSION QUESTIONS

1. In chapter one, what happens to make the author feel unworthy to be a Christian? Have you ever been tempted to think certain types of people are beyond God's love and acceptance? What types of people does Jesus welcome in the following passages: Luke 19:1–7; John 4:15–18, 25–26; Luke 7:36–39, 48–50?

2. In chapter two, what unwise choices does the author make? How do those choices make her feel? In chapter three, the author is on a quest to understand

the gospel message. What issues does she wrestle with in particular? What helps her understand the seriousness of sin? What does she know she must do?

3. In chapters four and five, what key things cause the author's faith to grow and mature? Do you believe studying God's Word is central to a growing relationship with God? If so, what steps can you take to spend more time in God's Word?

4. Three times in the book (in chapters seven, eight and thirteen), the author is challenged to surrender more of her life to God. What were those times and why were they so challenging? Each time, what convinced her to trust God and surrender herself?

5. In chapter fifteen, what parallels does the author make between her own life and the lives of the dorm girls? Do you believe God can still be at work in messy lives? Can you think of some Bible characters whose lives were messy, but God still used them?

6. In the epilogue, the author reflects on the life she now lives by faith in God. What conclusions does she make? Does surrendering your life to God's plans for you excite you or make you fearful? How might this story encourage you to trust God more? (See also Galatians 2:20; Romans 12:1; John 4:34; Luke 9:23.)

Appendix:

THE KRUNG AND BRAO

The Krung and Brao people groups who feature in Joelle's story are two of several hilltribe groups in north-east Cambodia. The Krung/Brao/Laveh comprise around 40,000 people in North East Cambodia and 50,000 in Laos. Until 1993, there were no Christians among them in Cambodia. Today there are over 500 believers in Cambodia and over 200 in Laos. They are distinct from the majority of Cambodians (the Khmer People group) in various ways.

They have their own language, which was unwritten, until Bible translators arrived 20 years ago and began to create an alphabet for them. They have their own religion – animism, rather than Buddhism. This includes their own tradition of animal sacrifice believed to protect them from sickness, disease, bad harvests and so on. The hilltribe people groups also have distinct cultures, with their own laws, village elders, traditional clothing, style of cooking, own ideas about courtship, marriage, and death. For example, people are buried with all their personal belongings, and sometimes even their motorbike!

As Joelle describes, the hilltribe people groups are subsistence farmers – growing rice and vegetables for their own consumption and growing cashew nuts as a cash crop which they sell to neighbouring Vietnam, and Thailand. They interact with Khmer people to buy and sell goods – but otherwise they live quite separately from the rest of the country. Several different tribal groups live in three north-east provinces in Cambodia – Ratanakiri, Mondulkiri, and Stung Treng. The different tribal groups exist alongside each other peacefully and sometimes intermarry. Sadly, because they are less well educated, people from tribal groups are often looked down on by the Khmer and tricked into giving up their land. Deforestation and land-grabbing is a problem in Ratanakiri and continues to threaten the existence of these tribal communities, plus the local wildlife.

Find out more about Cambodia and OMF's work there at omf.org/cambodia

We hope you've enjoyed Joelle's story of her journey to Cambodia and how God is using her there.

Joelle serves with OMF International, which was founded by James Hudson Taylor in 1865 as the China Inland Mission. We serve the Church and share the good news of Jesus Christ in all its fullness with countries across East Asia. We're for all Christians who want to be relevant in mission. We're a forward-thinking gospel-focused movement that pursues every avenue to reach East Asians for Jesus. In a changing world, we need to find the most effective means possible.

Today this looks like around 1,400 workers from 40 countries serving across East Asia. Their ministries vary from church planting to medical work, from sport to theological education. Each of them seeks to serve the Church and share the good news of Jesus Christ in all its fullness.

Wondering what to read next? **Ultimate Grace**, *OMF worker Levi Booth's true story of frisbee and faith in Japan, is part of the same series of short biographies.*

Find out more about OMF, hear from Joelle on our podcast and find more free resources at **omf.org/uk**

Heart for Asia. Hope for Billions.

 /omfinternationaluk   omf_uk   omf_uk